fondue

fondue

fiona smith

photography by william lingwood

RYLAND
PETERS
& SMALL
LONDON NEW YORK

First published in the United States in 2002
by Ryland Peters & Small, Inc.
519 Broadway, 5th Floor
New York, NY 10012
www.rylandpeters.com

10 9 8 7 6 5

ISBN 1 84172 341 X

Library of Congress
Cataloging-in-Publication Data

Smith, Fiona, 1968–
    Fondue / Fiona Smith ;
    photography by William Lingwood.
      p. cm.
    ISBN 1-84172-341-X
    1. Fondue. I. Title.

    TX825 .S63 2002
    641.8'1--dc21   2002024852
Printed in China

Notes

All spoon measurements are level.
All eggs are large, unless otherwise specified.
Uncooked or partially cooked eggs should not be
served to the very young, the very old, those with
compromised immune systems, or to pregnant
women.
The cooking medium for a fondue should be
heated thoroughly on top of the stove before
carefully transfering to the tabletop burner. Foods
cooked on metal skewers should be removed
from the skewers before eating.

Senior Designer Susan Downing
Commissioning Editor Elsa Petersen-Schepelern
Editor Jennifer Herman
Production Deborah Wehner
Art Director Gabriella Le Grazie
Publishing Director Alison Starling

Food Stylist Fiona Smith
Stylist Helen Trent
Photographer's Assistant Emma Bentham-Wood

contents

which fondue for you?

Fondue began life in the mountains of Switzerland, and is still part of the Swiss skiing holiday experience. It became the darling of the dining set in the 1950s, then again in the 1970s. Now, fondue has made a comeback under the fashionable guise of retro food—a reputation helped by the fact that fondue is actually fantastic. Versatile, easy to prepare, and delicious, it is one of the great convivial eating experiences.

The name comes from *fondu,* the French word for "melted." The original dish comprised several types of cheese, melted in a little white wine and Kirsch. Later introductions— not true fondues, since nothing is melted—were fondue bourguignonne (hot oil) and fondue chinoise (seafood or meat cooked in hot stock, based on the Mongolian hotpot).

Cheese fondue is made in an earthenware pot called a *caquelon,* but any heatproof earthenware or enameled cast iron pot is suitable, as they disperse the heat at a steady, even rate that prevents overheating. For oil- and stock-based fondues, cooked directly in the pot, you must keep the cooking medium at a very high temperature (boiling point for stock, or 400°F for oil). Copper, stainless steel, or enameled cast iron pots are the best—for oil, choose one with a splatter guard, narrow top, or semi-enclosed lid. Never use earthenware for oil fondues: it will not withstand such high temperatures.

Fondues, oils, and stocks should be made or heated at the stove and then transferred to the tabletop burner. Take extreme care when doing this. Oil should fill only one-third of the pot and stock two-thirds. If you are preparing the fondue in a different pot from the one you use to serve, heat the serving dish before adding the fondue so the temperature doesn't drop. Have the tabletop burner alight before the hot dish arrives.

If you need anything more to encourage conviviality
a piece of bread accidentally dropped into the fondue is
traditionally paid for with a kiss!

This is where it all began—the cheese fondue. The traditional Swiss fondue, from the canton of Neuchâtel, is made from Gruyère and Emmental cheeses. There are many slight variations of this classic recipe; some use arrowroot, potato starch, or cornstarch instead of all-purpose flour, sometimes this is combined with the cold wine first, or added later with the Kirsch. Whichever method you use, the end result will be delicious and creamy. The recipe, plus variations, follows— but the secrets of successful cheese fondue making include:

- If the fondue is too thick, stir in a little heated wine.

- If it is too thin, add more cheese or stir in a little cornstarch blended with wine.

- If the fondue separates, keep stirring—it should recover. If all else fails, add a few drops of lemon juice and stir vigorously—or mix 1 teaspoon cornstarch with 2 tablespoons wine, then stir into the cheese.

- Fresh or blanched vegetables for dipping may not be traditional, but they taste wonderful as an alternative to bread.

cheese fondues

neuchâtel fondue

Rub the cut side of the garlic around the inside of the fondue pot. Pour in the wine and bring it to a boil on top of the stove. Reduce the heat to simmering.

Put the grated cheese into a bowl, add the flour, and toss well. Gradually add the cheese to the wine, stirring constantly, and letting each addition melt into the wine.

When the mixture is creamy and smooth, add Kirsch and pepper to taste, then transfer the pot to its tabletop burner. Arrange the bread on serving platters.

To eat, spear a piece of bread on a fondue fork, then dip it into the cheese mixture, swirling the fork in a figure-of-eight to keep the fondue smooth.

Variations

Other Swiss cantons created their own variations, usually by substituting their local cheese and wine. Try it with your own local dry wines and Gruyère-style cheeses:

Fondue Fribourgeois Substitute 4 cups Fontina cheese, rind removed, finely chopped, for either the Gruyère or Emmental (see note on Vacherin Fribourgeois page 46).

Appenzeller Fondue Appenzeller, available in the US, is a cheese washed in spiced wine or cider. Use instead of the Gruyère and Emmental, and another dry white wine or hard cider instead of Neuchâtel. Serve with bread, apples, grapes, and endive.

Comté Fondue Comté, available in the US, is a big, rich, fruity, Gruyère-type, especially suitable for fondues. Use 8 cups instead of the Gruyère and Emmental.

Rosé Fondue is highly unconventional, said to have been invented by tourists in Switzerland who, finding themselves temporarily bereft of white wine, used what they had and came up with a funky pink version. Follow the recipe for Neuchâtel Fondue, substituting a light, dry rosé for the white wine. Not for traditionalists!

1 garlic clove, halved

1¼ cups dry white wine, such as Neuchâtel or Sauvignon Blanc

13 oz. Gruyère cheese, coarsely grated, about 4 cups

13 oz. Emmental cheese, coarsely grated, about 4 cups

1 tablespoon all-purpose flour

2–4 tablespoons Kirsch

freshly ground black pepper

to serve

2½ lb. crusty bread, cut into cubes (about 7–8 oz. per person)

serves 6

When I worked in Switzerland, this fondue was my favorite. The tomatoes cut through the richness of the cheese, and less wine is needed as a result. I use roasted tomatoes for a fuller flavor. The tomatoes should produce about 2 cups tomato purée: if not, add extra volume in the form of canned purée, tomato juice, or more wine.

roasted tomato fondue

Put the tomatoes cut side up onto a baking tray. Sprinkle with the herbs, salt, and olive oil. Roast in a preheated oven at 325°F for 1 hour. Remove from the oven, let cool, then remove any herb stalks. Transfer the tomatoes to a blender or food processor, together with any juices from the baking tray. Blend to a purée, adding a little of the wine if the mixture is too thick. Press through a strainer to remove the skins.

Rub the cut side of the garlic around the inside of the fondue pot. Add the tomato purée and wine and bring to a boil. Reduce the heat to simmering.

Put the grated cheese and flour into a bowl and toss with a fork. Gradually add to the simmering tomato broth, stirring constantly, letting each addition melt into the broth before adding the next. Season with pepper.

Arrange platters and bowls of the cooked potatoes, gherkins, and cocktail onions on the table. Carefully transfer the pot to its tabletop burner.

Each guest should take a share of the potatoes, ladle the hot fondue over the top, then eat with the gherkins and pickled onions.

12 large, ripe tomatoes, halved and seeded

a small bunch of oregano, thyme, or marjoram

1 teaspoon sea salt

2 tablespoons olive oil

¾ cup dry white wine

1 garlic clove, halved

1 lb. cheese, such as Gruyère, Emmental, Fontina, or raclette, or a mixture, grated, about 4½ cups

1 tablespoon all-purpose flour

freshly ground black pepper

to serve

2½ lb. new potatoes, boiled or roasted

1 jar baby gherkins, about 14 oz.

1 jar cocktail onions, about 14 oz.

a baking tray

serves 6

The Italian version of fondue is a speciality of the Valle d'Aosta in the northwest. It is made with Fontina cheese, enriched with egg yolks, then sprinkled decadently with shavings of white truffles from neighboring Piedmont. If you don't have a truffle to hand, a sprinkling of truffle oil will give a hint of the prized fragrance.

fonduta

Put the cornstarch into a small bowl, add 1 tablespoon of the milk, and stir until dissolved—this is called "slaking."

Put the remaining milk into the top section of a double boiler, then add the cheese and slaked cornstarch. Put over a saucepan of simmering water and heat, stirring constantly, until the cheese melts. Stir in the butter, if using, and remove from the heat.

Put the egg yolks into a bowl and beat lightly. Beat in a few tablespoons of the hot cheese mixture to warm the yolks. Pour this mixture back into the double boiler, stirring vigorously. Return the saucepan to the heat and continue stirring until the mixture thickens.

To serve, ladle the cheese mixture into preheated bowls and sprinkle with freshly ground white pepper and shavings of truffle, if using. Alternatively, sprinkle with a few drops of truffle oil. Serve the bowls surrounded by the prepared vegetables, with toast or cornbread triangles for dipping.

½ teaspoon cornstarch

1 cup milk

1 lb. Fontina cheese, chopped, about 5 cups

4 tablespoons unsalted butter (optional)

4 egg yolks

freshly ground white pepper

1 white truffle (optional) or truffle oil

to serve

steamed spring vegetables such as baby carrots, baby turnips, asparagus, fennel, and snowpeas, cut into bite-size pieces if necessary

toast or cornbread triangles

serves 6

Nothing to do with rabbits, of course. Many countries have a version of the perennially popular cheese melted on toast—French *croque monsieur*, Italian *mozzarella in carozza*, while this Welsh classic is a particularly creamy version. I also love the Swiss version—*croûte fromage*—slices of bread, layered into a heavily buttered dish, topped with a little wine and lashings of cheese, then baked until brown and bubbling.

welsh rabbit with mustard onions

Put the ale into a heavy saucepan and heat until simmering.

Put the cheese, mustard powder, and pepper into a bowl and toss well. Using a fork or wooden spoon, stir the mixture into the hot ale. Gradually stir in the butter until the mixture is smooth. (It may not be fully blended until the egg is added in the next step.)

Put the egg into a bowl and beat lightly. Beat in a few tablespoons of the hot cheese mixture to warm the egg, then stir the mixture into the cheese. Stir in the Worcestershire sauce. Simmer for a few minutes until the mixture thickens.

Put the toasted muffins onto 4 serving plates and top with bacon and asparagus, if using. Pour over the cheese mixture. The rabbits may be broiled to brown the cheese, or left plain. Serve with the mustard onions, if using.

Mustard onions Put the verjuice or vinegar and sugar into a small nonreactive saucepan and heat until dissolved. Bring to a boil and reduce by half, about 5 minutes. Remove from the heat and stir in the mustard and onions. Let marinate for at least 1 hour, then serve with the rabbit.

⅔ cup ale or amber beef

8 oz. sharp, aged Cheddar cheese, grated, about 2 cups

½ teaspoon dry mustard powder

a pinch of cayenne pepper

1 tablespoon unsalted butter

1 egg

1 teaspoon Worcestershire sauce

mustard onions (optional)

1 cup verjuice or white rice vinegar*

½ cup sugar

1 tablespoon grainy mustard

1 jar cocktail onions, rinsed thoroughly, about 14 oz.

to serve

4 English muffins or thick, toasted crusty bread

broiled bacon (optional)

blanched asparagus (optional)

serves 4

Verjuice, an acidic juice made from unripe grapes, is available in some gourmet stores. If unavailable, use white rice vinegar.

Raclette is an essential experience for all cheese lovers. Traditionally, huge half wheels of raclette cheese are heated beside an open fire. Periodically, the melted layer is scraped onto a plate and served with potatoes, pickled onions, and gherkins. Nowadays, special equipment is available for melting the cheese, ranging from large grills holding two halves of a wheel, to nifty tabletop versions with little broiler pans for individual servings, as here. If you don't own one, an ordinary broiler and pieces of nonstick parchment paper work very well too.

raclette

Preheat the raclette machine, if using, according to the manufacturer's instructions. Heat all serving plates in the oven. Arrange platters of potatoes, gherkins, and cocktail onions on the table.

To eat, each person should put a slice of cheese into one of the small raclette trays, heat until melted, then eat with the accompaniments.

If you don't have a raclette machine, preheat an overhead broiler until very hot and put 4 slices of cheese onto 4 pieces of parchment paper. When your guests are seated and ready, broil the cheese for about 2 minutes until bubbling. Using a metal spatula, scrape the cheese off the paper onto the hot dinner plate and serve as before.

4 oz. raclette cheese, or other melting cheese, cut into 4 slices

8 oz. new potatoes, boiled in their skins

4–8 small gherkins

4–8 cocktail onions, rinsed thoroughly

an electric raclette machine or 4 pieces nonstick parchment paper, 4^1/$_2$ inches square

a baking tray

serves 1

Although there is nothing "melted" about oil fondues, they have borne the name since their invention in Switzerland in the 1950s. The fondue bourguignonne is so popular that there are Swiss butchers specially trained to slice the best cuts of beef for the dish. Though this one is the grandaddy of them all, fondues are also delicious made with other meats, such as lamb, pork, and venison, poultry such as chicken and duck, and also with fish or seafood. They are a wonderful way to entertain casually. The traditional recipe for fondue bourguignonne follows—but the secrets of successful oil fondue cooking include:

- Oil fondues should be served in metal pots—copper, stainless steel, or cast iron.

- Have a heatproof surface between the fondue and the table. Marble, thick wood, or thick, felt-lined board are all suitable.

- It is a good idea to use wooden or bamboo skewers to cook food in oil. Metal skewers retain heat and are likely to burn your mouth. If you do use metal fondue forks, transfer the meat to a plate or onto a different fork before eating.

- The meat chosen should be a tender cut, such as tenderloin.

- The meat should be very finely sliced—freezing it for 2–3 hours before slicing will make this easier. If you prefer, the meat can be cubed.

- Season meat with salt and pepper just before cooking, or just after.

oil fondues

fondue bourguignonne

The meat for this dish should be very finely sliced. To make this easier, freeze the whole tenderloin for about 2–3 hours before slicing. Traditionally, this fondue is served with several mayonnaise-based sauces flavored with a spoonful of curry powder, mustard, tomato sauce, or horseradish. You could also serve sweet chile sauce, soy sauce, chutney, and pickles. I much prefer the deliciously different accompaniments on the next page: try Skordalia made with celery root and Green Salsa made with sorrel.

Dry the sliced beef well with paper towels, then arrange on a serving platter.

Fill a metal fondue pot one-third full with oil. Heat the oil to 375°F or until a cube of bread will brown in 30 seconds. Very carefully transfer the pot to its tabletop burner.

Each guest should spear or thread a piece of beef onto a skewer and dip it into the hot oil for about 30–60 seconds (if you thread the meat a little way up the skewer, it can rest on the bottom of the pot without sticking). Serve with dips, salad, and bread.

Mayonnaise dips To make mayonnaise, put 2 egg yolks and 1 whole egg (at room temperature) into a food processor. Add 2 teaspoons Dijon mustard, a pinch of salt, and 1 teaspoon lemon juice. Blend until smooth and creamy, then gradually pour in about 1½ cups peanut or safflower oil until the mixture is thick and creamy. Blend in another teaspoon of lemon juice, and 1–2 teaspoons warm water if the mixture is too thick. Divide between 4 small bowls and stir one of the following into each bowl; ½ teaspoon curry powder, 1 teaspoon hot mustard, 1 tablespoon tomato sauce, or 1 teaspoon horseradish sauce.

3 lb. beef tenderloin, finely sliced

peanut or safflower oil, about 3–5 cups, depending on the size of your fondue pot

sea salt and freshly ground black pepper

to serve, your choice of:

flavored mayonnaise dips

Skordalia (opposite)

Green Salsa (opposite)

salads

crusty bread

serves 6

Skordalia is a garlicky sauce from Greece, usually made with potato, or walnuts and bread. Though not traditional, it is very good made with potato, celery root, or parsnip.

Cut the potato and celery root into even chunks. Put into a saucepan, cover with water, bring to a boil, cover with a lid, and simmer until tender. Drain, return to the pan, and cover with a dish cloth to dry out for 5 minutes.

Mash until smooth, then beat in the garlic, salt, and egg yolk with a wooden spoon. Gradually beat in the oil, then the lemon juice. If the mixture is too thick, add a little warm water. Serve with the fondue.

8 oz. boiling potatoes, about 2 medium

10 oz. celery root, about 8 oz. after peeling

2–3 garlic cloves, crushed

1/2 teaspoon salt

1 egg yolk

1/2 cup extra virgin olive oil

juice of 1/2 lemon

makes 2 cups

Green salsa is also good with fondues. This one is made with lemony sorrel leaves. There is really no substitute for them, but arugula salsa would be delicious.

Grate the zest of the limes and transfer to a small food processor or use a large mortar and pestle. Add the scallions, garlic, and parsley and work to a coarse mixture. Add the juice of 1 lime, then the sorrel and oil to form a coarse green paste. Add salt and pepper to taste.

2 limes

4 scallions, finely sliced

2 garlic cloves, crushed

a small bunch of flat-leaf parsley, finely chopped, about 1/2 cup

a large bunch of sorrel, about 1 oz., finely chopped

2 tablespoons olive oil

sea salt and freshly ground black pepper

makes 1/2 cup

Lamb makes a great variation on the classic beef fondue. Again, to make the lamb easier to slice, freeze it for about 1 hour first. Baharat is a fragrant Middle Eastern spice mix—it can be a combination of many herbs, spices, and flowers, and I have added nuts to soften the blend.

lamb fondue
with toasted baharat

To make the baharat, put the almonds and pistachios into a dry skillet and toast for a few minutes until brown. Let cool, then transfer to a food processor and grind coarsely. Toast the sesame seeds in the skillet, then add to the processor and pulse briefly.

Put the black peppercorns, cumin, coriander seeds, and crumbled cinnamon into the skillet and dry-toast for a few minutes until fragrant. Transfer to a spice grinder, add the paprika and nutmeg, and grind to a powder. Alternatively, use a mortar and pestle. Transfer to an airtight container, add the nut and seed mixture, and shake well. The mixture will keep for 1 month, and can be used to flavor meats or vegetables, or as a dip with bread and oil.

To prepare the fondue, pat the lamb dry with paper towels and arrange on a serving platter. Spoon the baharat into 6 small bowls.

Fill a metal fondue pot one-third full with oil and heat to 375°F or until a cube of bread browns in 30 seconds. Very carefully transfer the pot to its tabletop burner. Each guest should spear or thread a piece of lamb onto a skewer and dip into the hot oil for 15–30 seconds. Dip the hot lamb into the baharat, then eat. Alternatively, make flatbread wraps with the lamb, hummus, salad, and yogurt.

3 lb. boneless leg of lamb or loin meat, finely sliced

3–5 cups peanut or safflower oil

baharat spice mix

4 oz. blanched almonds, 2/3 cup

4 oz. shelled pistachios, 2/3 cup

1/4 cup sesame seeds

1 tablespoon black peppercorns

1 1/2 tablespoons cumin seeds

1 tablespoon coriander seeds

2 cinnamon sticks, crumbled

1–2 tablespoons sweet paprika

1/2 teaspoon grated nutmeg

to serve (optional)

flatbreads

hummus

salad leaves

plain yogurt

serves 6

Fondues don't have to be Swiss—they are also a fabulously easy way to throw a North African dinner party. Serve platters of couscous tossed with herbs and sautéed vegetables, pass around bowls of relish, then have your guests cook their own chicken and duck skewers. The rendered duck fat added to the cooking oil gives a wonderful depth of flavor.

chicken and duck fondue
with tunisian relish

To make the Tunisian relish, chop the tomatoes and preserved lemon peel very finely and put into a bowl. Stir in the harissa or tomato paste, cilantro, and olive oil. Season with salt and set aside for a few hours to develop the flavors.

Cut the chicken and duck into $1/2$-inch strips and thread the strips onto the skewers, about 2 oz. per skewer, leaving about $1^1/2$ inches at the end, so it can rest it on the bottom of the pot without sticking. Arrange on a serving platter. Set platters of couscous and bowls of Tunisian relish on the table.

Fill a metal fondue pot one-third full with oil and add the duck fat trimmings. Heat the oil to 350°F or until a cube of bread browns in 40 seconds. Very carefully transfer the pot to its tabletop burner. Remove the duck fat when it becomes brown.

Guests should cook the skewers of duck and chicken in the hot oil for 2 minutes, then eat with the couscous and relish.

2 lb. skinless, boneless chicken breasts or thighs

1 lb. duck breast, with the fat trimmed and reserved

3–5 cups peanut or safflower oil

couscous tossed with herbs and sautéed vegetables, to serve

tunisian relish

4 large tomatoes, peeled and seeded

the peel of 1 preserved lemon*

2 tablespoons harissa* or tomato paste

a large handful of fresh cilantro, chopped

2 tablespoons olive oil

sea salt

serves 6

*Available in Middle Eastern stores.

A sizzling, very adaptable appetizer. Serve it with this almond and basil dip for a Mediterranean feast—or, if you substitute Thai basil and lime, you have the perfect appetizer for an Asian meal. The tentacles of the squid look most dramatic, but if they are unavailable, you can use just the bodies.

shrimp and calamari skewers
with almond and basil dip

To make the almond and basil dip, put the almonds and lemon or lime zest into a food processor and grind coarsely. Add the basil and parsley and grind again. Add salt to taste and set aside.

If the squid are whole, clean them by pulling the tentacles out of the body, then cut off the rosette of tentacles and press out the tiny hard piece in the middle. Pull the pen (the transparent wafer) out of the body and discard it. Remove the thin purplish skin if preferred. Rinse the bodies, pat dry, and cut in half. Using a sharp knife or Chinese cleaver, lightly score the inside surface of the bodies with criss-cross hatching.

Peel and devein the shrimp, leaving the tails attached. Thread a shrimp or a piece of squid onto each long bamboo skewer. Arrange platters of seafood and bowls of dip on the table.

Fill a metal fondue pot no more than one-third full with the oil. Put the pot on top of the stove and heat the oil to 375°F or until a cube of bread browns in 30 seconds. Very carefully transfer the pot to its tabletop burner.

Guests should cook the skewers in the hot oil for about 1 minute, then roll the skewers in the almond and basil dip and eat!

1 lb. small squid, about 16

1 lb. large shrimp

3–5 cups peanut or safflower oil

almond and basil dip

3 oz. blanched almonds, about 2 cups

finely grated zest of 2 lemons or 4 limes

a small bunch of basil, about 1/2 cup leaves

a small bunch of flat-leaf parsley, about 1/2 cup leaves

sea salt

serves 8 as a appetizer

Fritto misto and tempura are fantastic ways to serve vegetables, but since they are best straight from the pan, they can be a bit of a hassle to cook and serve. Often the cook gets stuck in the kitchen while other people enjoy themselves. Served as a fondue, it becomes a happy, communal task, and the taste couldn't get any fresher.

crispy vegetable fondue
with citrus dipping sauce

Prepare all the vegetables, pat dry with paper towels, and arrange on serving platters. To prepare the sweet potatoes, cut into $\frac{1}{2}$-inch slices, then cut these into quarters. Put into a saucepan, add cold water to cover, bring to a boil, then drain and cool under cold water. Dry well. Cut each pepper lengthwise into 12 and discard the seeds.

Put all the dipping sauce ingredients into a bowl and mix well. Divide between 6 small bowls. Fill a metal fondue pot one-third full with the oil and heat to 400°F, or until a piece of bread turns golden in 25 seconds.

Put the egg yolks, olive oil, and $\frac{3}{4}$ cup ice water into a bowl and beat well. Beat in the salt and flour to form a smooth batter: do not overmix. Beat the egg whites in a second bowl, until stiff but not dry, then fold into the batter.

Transfer the hot oil carefully to its tabletop burner to keep hot (make sure the temperature doesn't drop or the vegetables will be greasy).

Guests should spear the pieces of vegetable onto fondue forks, dip into the batter, then cook for 2–3 minutes until golden and crispy. Serve with the dip.

2 sweet potatoes

1 small red bell pepper

1 small yellow bell pepper

1 small head of broccoli, divided into 12 pieces

4 zucchini, cut diagonally into $\frac{1}{2}$-inch slices

12 mushrooms, halved

2 eggs, separated

1 tablespoon olive oil

1 cup all-purpose flour

a pinch of salt

3–5 cups peanut or safflower oil

citrus dipping sauce

$\frac{1}{2}$ cup lime or lemon juice

1 tablespoon honey

1 tablespoon grainy mustard

1 tablespoon Asian fish sauce

sea salt and freshly ground black pepper

serves 6

Bagna cauda is a rich garlic and anchovy dip from Piedmont in the north of Italy. It isn't strictly a fondue, but is traditionally served hot from a small fondue dish. Serve with a selection of vegetables, including endive leaves, fennel, celery, and cardoons (a relative of the artichoke). Other choices are peppers, carrots, mushrooms, cherry tomatoes, cauliflower, and regular artichoke hearts. It's also marvelous just with bread, or the Walnut Grissini on page 43.

bagna cauda

¾ cup extra virgin olive oil

4–5 garlic cloves, crushed

12 anchovy fillets, mashed, about 2–3 oz.

¼ cup walnut paste or almond butter*, or 2 tablespoons each of walnut oil and butter

to serve

a selection of vegetables, trimmed and cut into pieces

crusty bread (optional)

serves 4–6 as a appetizer

*Available at natural food stores.

Put the oil, garlic, and anchovies into a small saucepan and heat gently, taking care not to brown the garlic. Stir in the walnut paste or walnut oil and butter and cook for 2–3 minutes. Transfer to a bowl and set over a table candle burner to keep the mixture warm. Serve with the vegetables and bread, if using, for dipping.

Variation

Creamy Bagna Cauda Put 1¾ cups light cream into a small saucepan and bring to a boil. Simmer until reduced by half—about 5 minutes. Put 1 tablespoon butter into a small fondue pot and melt over a low heat. Add 12 anchovy fillets, finely chopped, and 4 crushed garlic cloves and cook briefly, mashing together and taking care not to let the garlic brown. Stir in the reduced cream and transfer the bowl to its tabletop burner to keep warm. Serve with vegetables and bread.

Hot stock is a wonderful cooking medium for seafood—this one is infused with saffron and tomato to give a delicious broth with Mediterranean flavor.

fish and seafood
in saffron and tomato broth

To make the broth, put the oil into a large saucepan and heat gently. Add the garlic, onion, and chile and sauté for a few minutes. Add the tomatoes, anchovies, white wine, bay leaves, orange peel, and 1 cup water and bring to a boil. Let simmer for 20 minutes, then add the saffron and its soaking water and simmer for a further 10 minutes.

To make the rouille, moisten the baguette with a little broth. Put it into a small food processor, then add the egg yolk, garlic, saffron, and chile and blend well. With the machine running, slowly pour in the olive oil to form a paste. Add 1–2 teaspoons broth, stir well, then transfer to 6 small bowls.

Strain the broth into a metal fondue pot until two-thirds full, adding extra water if necessary. Season with salt and pepper and return to a boil. Transfer the pot to its tabletop burner and keep boiling.

Guests should spear pieces of fish and shellfish with their fondue forks, lower into the boiling broth, and cook for 30–60 seconds. Serve with rouille and crusty bread. The broth can be served as a soup, either after the fondue, or next day.

12 uncooked jumbo shrimp, peeled

12 scallops

1 lb. monkfish, cut into bite-size chunks

1 lb. salmon fillet, cut into bite-size chunks

crusty bread, to serve

saffron and tomato broth

1 tablespoon olive oil

2 garlic cloves, sliced

1 onion, sliced

1 red chile, seeded and sliced

1 lb. tomatoes, finely chopped

2 anchovy fillets, chopped (optional)

1 cup dry white wine

2 bay leaves

1 long piece of orange peel, fresh or dried

$\frac{1}{2}$ teaspoon saffron threads, soaked in $\frac{1}{4}$ cup boiling water for 15 minutes

sea salt and freshly ground black pepper

rouille

1 thick slice of baguette loaf

1 egg yolk

2 garlic cloves, crushed

$\frac{1}{4}$ teaspoon saffron powder

$\frac{1}{2}$ teaspoon finely chopped fresh chile

$\frac{1}{4}$ cup olive oil

serves 6

stock fondues

The aniseed flavors of Pernod and chervil complement the delicate lobster and sole in this hotpot-style fondue. If you can't get lobster, try shrimp, scallops, or other firm white fish. Using the lobster shells in the court bouillon will give it exceptional flavor.

lobster and sole
in anise-scented court bouillon

Cut the sole fillets in half lengthwise. Put a tiny bunch of chervil at the end of each and roll up. Secure each roll with a long skewer. Spear the pieces of lobster onto skewers.

To make the court bouillon, put the oil into a large saucepan, heat gently, then add the carrots, celery, and leek and sauté until soft, about 5 minutes. Add 2 quarts water, the bay leaf, parsley, fennel seeds, and fish bones and shells, and simmer for 30 minutes. Strain into a metal fondue pot, add enough water to fill the pot two-thirds full, then bring to a boil on top of the stove. Add the Pernod and salt to taste. Transfer the pot to its tabletop burner and keep boiling.

Guests should cook the lobster and sole rolls in the boiling stock for 30–60 seconds. Suitable accompaniments, especially for an elegant summer meal, are boiled new potatoes, a green salad, and some lemon mayonnaise or melted butter for dipping.

2 small sole fillets, skinned, about 1½ lb.

a small bunch of chervil

about 1 lb. lobster tails, with shell if possible, shrimp or scallops, or monkfish, cut into bite-size pieces

pernod court bouillon

2 tablespoons olive oil

2 small carrots, finely chopped

1 celery stalk, finely chopped

1 small leek, sliced

1 bay leaf

a small bunch of parsley

1 tablespoon fennel seeds

1½ lb. fish bones, including lobster or langoustine shells if possible

⅓ cup Pernod

salt

to serve

boiled new potatoes

green salad

lemon mayonnaise or melted butter

serves 6

Wrapping chicken in vine leaves not only infuses the chicken with flavor, it also looks more stylish. I have used preserved lemons because I love their intense flavor—substitute lemon zest if unavailable.

chicken in vine leaves
with lemon-scented broth

To make the broth, put all the broth ingredients except the lemon and salt into a large saucepan. Add 2 quarts water, bring to a boil, reduce to a simmer, and cook for 45 minutes, skimming off any foam that forms on the top. Strain into a metal fondue pot. Remove any meat from the chicken bones, shred, then add to the stock. Discard the bones. Add the preserved lemon and salt to taste and enough water to fill the pot two-thirds full.

Butterfly each chicken breast by slicing through to about ½ inch from the edge and opening out. Using a meat mallet or rolling pin, gently flatten the chicken to ½ inch thick.

Roast the peppers under a very hot broiler or in the flames of a gas burner, until blackened all over. Transfer to a large bowl and cover with plastic wrap. Let steam for about 10 minutes, then peel off the skin. Split the peppers into quarters and discard the stalks and seeds.

Arrange 4 vine leaves in an overlapping square. Top with a piece of chicken and 2 quarters of pepper. Roll up tightly and slice into 6 rounds, like sushi. Secure each piece with a long skewer, sliding the chicken about a quarter of the way up the skewer. Repeat until all the chicken has been used. Refrigerate until needed.

Bring the broth to a boil on top of the stove, then transfer the pot to its tabletop burner. Guests dip the chicken rolls into the broth and cook for 5–6 minutes. Serve with rice and sauces.

6 boneless, skinless chicken breasts

3 red or yellow bell peppers

4 oz. preserved vine leaves, about 24, drained

lemon-scented broth

1 lb. chicken wings

3 garlic cloves

1 onion, halved

2 bay leaves

½ tablespoon black peppercorns

a large bunch of parsley, about 1 oz. (¾ cup chopped)

1 preserved lemon, washed, seeded, and finely chopped*

sea salt

to serve

boiled rice

sauces, such as hummus, pesto, and sweet chile

serves 6

Available in Middle Eastern stores.

The beef is prepared in the same way as fondue bourguignonne on page 22—freeze the tenderloin for about 2–3 hours first to make it easier to slice thinly. The stock is delicious: if you have any left over, it can be used in soups and it also freezes very well. If you don't have any fresh beets available, the precooked kind makes a speedy substitute.

beef with horseradish
in red wine and juniper stock

To make the stock, put the beef bones into a roasting pan and cook in a preheated oven at 400°F for 30 minutes. Remove and transfer to a large saucepan. Add the onion, carrots, celery, and 3 quarts water and bring to a boil. Simmer for 1 hour, skimming any foam off the top. Strain and discard the solids.

Meanwhile, to make the relish, put the beets into a roasting pan and cook in a preheated oven at 350°F for 40 minutes or until tender. Cool slightly and peel. Grate coarsely into a bowl and stir in the olive oil, horseradish, salt, and pepper.

Put the red wine into a metal fondue pot and bring to a boil on top of the stove. Boil until reduced by half, then add the juniper berries, cloves, star anise, peppercorns, and strained stock. Add salt to taste. Return to a boil and transfer the pot to its tabletop burner to keep simmering. Put platters of sliced beef and toasted Italian bread and a bowl of relish on the table.

Guests should thread a slice of beef onto a fondue fork and cook in the simmering stock for 30–60 seconds. Eat the beef on the toasted bread with a spoonful of the beet and horseradish relish.

2$^1/_2$ lb. beef tenderloin, finely sliced
toasted Italian bread, to serve

red wine and juniper stock

2 lb. beef bones
1 onion, coarsely chopped
2 carrots, coarsely chopped
1 celery stalk
1 cup red wine
1 tablespoon juniper berries
$^1/_2$ teaspoon whole cloves
2–3 whole star anise
1 teaspoon black peppercorns
sea salt

beet and horseradish relish

6 beets, raw and unpeeled, scrubbed well
2 tablespoons olive oil
3 tablespoons horseradish sauce
sea salt and freshly ground black pepper

serves 6

modern fondues

Blue cheese, fresh walnuts, and juicy pears make a delicious combination. This fondue is perfect served as a appetizer with asparagus, or as a dessert with pears.

blue cheese fondue
with walnut grissini

To make the walnut grissini, put the flour, yeast, walnuts, and salt into a food processor fitted with a plastic blade. With the machine running, add the oil and $3/4$ cup water through the feed tube. Process in 15-second bursts until it forms a soft mass. Turn out onto a floured board and knead for 2 minutes. Put the dough into an oiled bowl, cover, and let rest for 1 hour.

Knead again lightly and flatten to a rectangle about 16 x 6 inches. Cut crosswise into $1/2$-inch strips, roll and stretch out each strip to about 12 inches, and transfer to a baking tray (you will need to bake in two batches). Cook in a preheated oven at 400°F for 16–18 minutes. Remove from the oven and let cool on a wire rack. Serve immediately or store in an airtight container for up to 1 week.

To prepare the fondue, pour the wine into a small metal fondue pot and heat until simmering. Gradually stir in the blue cheese, then the cornstarch mixture, stirring constantly until smooth. Transfer the pot to its tabletop burner and serve with Walnut Grissini and pears or asparagus.

$1/2$ cup sweet white wine such as Gewürztraminer

14 oz. creamy blue cheese, such as Gorgonzola or Roquefort, coarsely chopped

1 teaspoon cornstarch mixed with 1 tablespoon of the wine

walnut grissini

3 cups all-purpose flour, plus extra for rolling

1 package ($1/4$ oz.) active dry yeast

3 oz. fresh walnuts, about $1/4$ cup

1 teaspoon sea salt

2 tablespoons walnut oil, plus extra for the bowl

to serve

4–6 ripe pears, quartered, or 24 asparagus spears, lightly cooked

a baking tray

serves 6

Roasted red bell peppers, like the tomatoes in the fondue on page 12, have a sweet acidity that blends well with cheese. I like to serve this fondue over roasted pumpkin sprinkled with paprika, but boiled potatoes are also good.

roasted red bell pepper
cheese fondue

Roast the bell peppers under a very hot broiler or in the flames of a gas burner, until blackened all over. Transfer to a large bowl and cover with plastic wrap. Let steam for about 10 minutes, then peel off the skin. Halve the peppers and discard the stalks and seeds. Finely slice and reserve one pepper for serving and put the remainder into a food processor. Add the wine or tomato juice and blend to a coarse purée.

Heat the olive oil in a fondue pot and sauté the scallions and jalapeño chiles until soft, about 5–7 minutes. Stir in the pepper purée and simmer for 5 minutes. Stir in the cream and heat but do not boil. Remove from the heat.

Add the cream cheese, stir until melted, and return to the heat. Put the queso fresco or asadero cheese and flour into a bowl, toss well, then gradually add to the fondue, stirring constantly.

Transfer the fondue pot to its tabletop burner and sprinkle with the reserved sliced pepper. Guests should ladle the pepper cheese over the pumpkin and eat with tortillas or bread. Quince paste (*membrillo* in Spanish) makes an interesting accompaniment.

6 red bell peppers

$\frac{1}{2}$ cup dry white wine or tomato juice

2 tablespoons olive oil

6 scallions, finely chopped

3 fresh jalapeño chiles, seeded and finely chopped

$\frac{3}{4}$ cup light cream

4 oz. cream cheese, cut or broken into small pieces, about $\frac{1}{2}$ cup

8 oz. Mexican queso fresco or asadero cheese, crumbled or grated, about 2 cups

1 tablespoon all-purpose flour

to serve

roasted pumpkin sprinkled with paprika

soft tortillas or sourdough bread

quince paste (optional)

serves 6

Vacherin is one of the world's great cheeses. The three varieties are unpasteurized, so are difficult to find in America. Vacherin Fribourgeois, the one used in cooking and to make fondues, is a little less sweet than Emmental, and so is perfect with the sweetness of caramelized shallots. Fontina or raclette cheese are suitable alternatives. I have kept the name for tradition's sake.

vacherin fondue
with caramelized shallots

Put the butter into a cheese fondue pot and melt over medium heat. Add the shallots, reduce the heat to low, and cook for 10 minutes. Stir in the sugar, then the vinegar, and cook for a further 10 minutes. Remove a few shallots and set aside for serving.

Pour in the wine, bring to a boil, then reduce to a simmer.

Put the Gruyère and flour into a bowl and toss well. Gradually add the cheese to the simmering fondue mixture, stirring constantly. Stir in the Fontina or raclette, then the port, if using.

Transfer the fondue pot to its tabletop burner, add the reserved shallots, and serve the fondue with cubes of bread and vegetables for dipping. Alternatively, put slices of baguette into 6 individual bowls and ladle the fondue over the top.

2 tablespoons butter
or olive oil

10 oz. shallots, finely sliced

2 teaspoons light brown sugar

2 tablespoons balsamic or
cider vinegar

2 cups dry white wine

10 oz. Gruyère cheese, grated,
about 1¼ cups

1 tablespoon all-purpose flour

10 oz. Fontina or raclette
cheese, grated, about 1¼ cups

2 tablespoons port wine
(optional)

to serve

bread such as sourdough or
baguette, cubed

fresh vegetables

cherry tomatoes

serves 6

In France, a brandade is a thick, creamy purée made with salt cod. With a few alterations, it makes a wonderful fondue. Because preparing salt cod can be a time-consuming business, I have used a smoked fish—not traditional but still good. Serve it in a fondue pot or, as I have done, in individual dishes.

individual
smoked fish fondues

Put the flaked fish and garlic into a food processor. With the motor running, pour in the olive oil to form a paste. Add the cream cheese and pulse until just mixed.*

Stir in the milk and lemon juice. Taste, then season with salt and pepper (take care, because the fish is often quite salty).

Spoon into the 8 ramekins and bake in a preheated oven at 350°F for 20 minutes until hot and bubbly.

Serve with the sugarsnap peas, hard-cooked eggs, and toast for dipping.

*Note To serve the smoked fish fondue in a pot, transfer the mixture at this point to the pot, and heat gently, stirring. Add the milk, then the lemon juice. Transfer the pot to its tabletop burner to keep warm. If the mixture is too thick, add a splash of dry white wine. Serve as in the main recipe.

12 oz. white fish fillets, such as snapper or cod, skinned and cut into cubes*

12 oz. smoked salmon, skinned and cut into cubes*

2 garlic cloves, crushed

1/2 cup virgin olive oil

8 oz. cream cheese, about 1 cup

1/2 cup milk

2 tablespoons lemon juice

sea salt and freshly ground black pepper

to serve, your choice of:

sugarsnap peas

hard-cooked eggs, quartered

strips of toast

8 small ramekins, buttered

serves 8

*If available, substitute 1 1/2 lb. smoked cod or haddock, skinned and cubed.

A simple, delicious appetizer. I always use fresh crab, but frozen lumpmeat or flaked is also good. You could also serve this as a dip at parties—just make sure the burner and pot are safely fixed on the serving platter.

hot ginger
and crab fondue

Using a mandoline or vegetable peeler, finely slice the Brazil nuts into shavings. Set aside.

Put the cream cheese and sherry into a small fondue pot and stir until smooth. Add the scallions and ginger, and heat gently until bubbling. Stir in the crabmeat, then sprinkle with the nut shavings.

Transfer the pot to its tabletop burner to keep warm and serve with crackers, Walnut Grissini, and toast for dipping.

2 oz. Brazil nuts or flaked almonds, about ⅓ cup

8 oz. cream cheese, about 1 cup

¼ cup sherry

4 scallions, finely sliced

1 tablespoon grated fresh ginger

8 oz. crabmeat, about 2 cups

to serve

crackers

Walnut Grissini (page 43)

toast, cut into strips or triangles

serves 8 as an appetizer

When I was in Switzerland, potato rösti (pancakes) were one of my favorite dishes. I have an apple version here, the perfect foil for a Cheddar fondue, flavored with the fiery apple brandy, Calvados. Cheddar cheeses are traditionally served with apples, so it's a perfect match.

cheddar and calvados fondue
with apple rösti

To make the rösti, grate the potatoes on the coarse side of a box grater, put into a bowl, cover with water, and let soak for 10 minutes. Drain in a colander, then transfer to a clean dish cloth and squeeze out very well. Grate the apples into the bowl, add the lemon juice to stop discoloration, toss well, then squeeze out in a dish cloth. Put the potato and apple back into a clean dry bowl, add the salt and pepper, and mix well.

Put half the oil into the skillet, heat well, add the potato mixture, press down with a fork, and reduce the heat to medium-low. Cook for 10 minutes until brown, loosen with a spatula, then turn out onto a large plate. Wipe around the skillet, add the remaining oil, and slide the rösti back into the skillet. Cook for a further 10 minutes until cooked through. Keep warm in the oven until needed.

Pour the cider into a fondue pot and bring to a boil. Reduce the heat to a simmer. Put the grated cheese and flour into a bowl and toss with a fork. Gradually add the cheese to the pot, stirring constantly, letting each addition melt into the cider. When creamy and smooth, add the Calvados and pepper to taste.

To serve, slice the rösti into 12, put 2 wedges onto each warmed plate, and top with bacon, if using, and a ladle of the hot fondue.

¾ cup hard cider

13 oz. Cheddar cheese, coarsely grated, about 3 cups

1 tablespoon all-purpose flour

¼ cup Calvados or brandy

freshly ground black pepper

crisp sautéed bacon, to serve (optional)

apple rösti

3–4 potatoes, about 1 lb.

2 apples, about 10 oz., peeled

juice of 1 lemon

½ teaspoon sea salt

freshly ground black pepper

1 tablespoon olive oil

a nonstick skillet, 9-inch diameter

serves 6

Sweet fondues make an easy, friendly dessert. Any sweet cookies are good for dipping, but my favorites are churros—the delicious doughnuts the Spanish serve with hot chocolate drinks.

bittersweet chocolate fondue
with spanish churros

To prepare the fondue, put the chocolate into the top of a double boiler, add the cream, pepper flakes, liqueur, if using, and orange zest and juice. Heat over simmering water and stir until melted and smooth. Transfer to a warmed fondue pot set over its tabletop burner. Serve with fruit and churros or other cookies.

Churros Put the milk into a saucepan and heat to boiling point. Remove from the heat and quickly stir in all the flour. Beat in the egg and salt and let cool to room temperature.

Put the cinnamon, star anise, and 2 tablespoons of the sugar into a spice grinder or clean coffee grinder and grind to a powder. Alternatively, use a mortar and pestle. Sift to remove any large pieces. Transfer to a shallow bowl and stir in the remaining sugar.

Fill a saucepan or deep-fryer no more than one-third full with the oil. Heat the oil to 375°F or until a cube of bread browns in 30 seconds.

Fill a piping bag or cookie press with the mixture. Pipe 4-inch lengths of dough into the hot oil and cook for 4 minutes until golden on all sides. Drain on paper towels. While still warm, roll the churros in the cinnamon sugar mixture, then serve with the fondue. The churros are best eaten immediately or they will lose their crispness. If made in advance, reheat for 5 minutes in a preheated oven at 400°F before serving.

10 squares (10 oz.) bittersweet chocolate

1/2 cup cream

1/4 teaspoon hot red pepper flakes (optional)

2 tablespoons orange liqueur such as Cointreau (optional)

finely grated zest and juice of 2 oranges

to serve

your choice of sweet cookies, churros, and fresh fruits

churros

1¾ cups milk

1½ cups self-rising flour

1 egg, lightly beaten

1/2 teaspoon salt

1 cinnamon stick, crumbled

2 whole star anise

1/2 cup plus 1 tablespoon sugar

3 cups peanut or safflower oil.

a strong piping bag fitted with a large star nozzle, or cookie press

serves 6

sweet fondues

Bread and chocolate are a favorite combination in Switzerland, and this spin on the classic *croûte fromage* makes a great finale for a meal. Serve like a crumble or a cobbler, with custard or cream.

croûte chocolat

Arrange the slices of panettone in overlapping rows in the prepared baking dish. Insert the slices of banana and strawberry halves between the slices of panettone. Sprinkle with the citrus liqueur or orange juice, then add a layer of grated chocolate.

Bake in a preheated oven at 400°F for about 20 minutes, until well heated through and the chocolate has melted.

Serve with your choice of custard, cream, ice cream, or yogurt.

1 tablespoon butter

12 slices panettone, brioche, or dried fruit bread, about 4 inches square, ½ inch thick

2 bananas, sliced

8 oz. strawberries, hulled and halved, about 2 cups

¼ cup citrus liqueur, such as Cointreau, Limoncello, or Grand Marnier, or fresh orange juice

4–7 squares (4–7 oz.) white or bittersweet chocolate, grated

custard, fresh cream, ice cream, crème fraîche, or plain yogurt, to serve

a baking dish, about 8 x 6 inches, well buttered

serves 6

There are some who argue that white chocolate isn't "real" chocolate. I don't think it matters at all—it's delicious and looks beautiful. I based this recipe on some heavenly truffles I once tasted, made from white chocolate, lemon, and gin.

white chocolate fondue
with lemon and gin

Wash the strawberries, but do not hull them, then pat them dry with paper towels (if you hull them before washing, they will fill with water).

Thread a few blueberries onto small skewers. Arrange the blueberry skewers, strawberries, and sweet cookies on a serving plate.

Put the cream, gin, and lemon zest into the top of a double boiler set over simmering water and heat gently. Add the chocolate and stir until smooth. Transfer to a fondue pot and set over its tabletop burner,* then serve with the fruit and cookies.

*Note White chocolate is very thin when hot. If you would prefer a thicker fondue, turn off the burner, let cool, then chill for 1–2 hours.

$\frac{1}{3}$ cup heavy cream

3 tablespoons gin

very finely grated zest of 2 lemons

8 squares (8 oz.) best-quality white chocolate, chopped

to serve

1 lb. strawberries, about 4 cups

8 oz. blueberries, about 2 cups

sweet cookies such as ladyfingers, madeleines, or amaretti

serves 6

This beautifully scented fondue is made using a method similar to zabaglione—it can be served in a fondue pot, or as individual servings in tea glasses or bowls.

orange and cardamom fondue
with caramel grapes and dates

Divide the grapes into small bunches and spear each date with a bamboo skewer. Put the sugar into a heavy saucepan, add ⅓ cup water, and heat, stirring until the sugar has dissolved. Bring to a boil but do not stir—you can gently swirl the pan around so the sugar colors evenly. Boil for 5 minutes

until the sugar is a golden caramel. Remove from the heat and, working quickly, dip bunches of grapes and dates into the caramel. Put onto a plate or tray lined with baking parchment, let dry, then transfer to a serving platter or small plates.

To prepare the fondue, put the cardamom into a skillet and heat for 3 minutes until aromatic. Crush the pods with a mortar and pestle. Put into a small saucepan, add the orange juice and zest, and simmer gently for 2 minutes. Remove from the heat, let cool, then strain and measure out ⅓ cup.

Put the egg yolks, egg, and sugar into a heatproof bowl set over simmering water. Using electric beaters, beat the mixture for 10 minutes until thick and mousse-like. Gradually beat in the orange and cardamom mixture and continue beating for 5 minutes. Pour into a fondue pot and set over its tabletop burner, or into individual glasses, then serve with the dates and grapes.

2 teaspoons green cardamom pods

very finely grated zest and ½ cup freshly squeezed juice of 1 large orange

2 egg yolks

1 whole egg

¼ heaping cup sugar

caramel grapes and dates

1 lb. seedless grapes, about 3 cups

8 oz. fresh or semi-dried dates, about 30

⅓ cup sugar

serves 4

Rosewater is sold in Middle Eastern stores and supermarket baking sections. If unavailable, use Amaretto liqueur or vanilla. I like to toast and grind the almonds myself, so they are fresher and have more texture.

mascarpone and rose fondue
with almond syrup cookies

To make the almond syrup cookies, put the toasted almonds into a food processor and grind to a coarse mixture. Transfer to a bowl, then add the sugar and lemon zest. Make a well in the center, add the egg, and mix well.

Transfer to a well-floured work surface and shape into a flat log, 10 x 3 x ¾ inch deep. Cut 20–24 slices. Arrange apart on the prepared baking tray. Transfer to a preheated oven and cook at 350°F for 18 minutes. Remove from the oven and let cool on a wire rack.

Meanwhile, put the remaining sugar and the lemon juice into a saucepan and bring to a boil. Simmer for 3 minutes until syrupy. Cool, then drizzle over the cookies.

Put the mascarpone, confectioners' sugar, and Marsala or cream into a small heatproof bowl set over a saucepan of simmering water and heat, stirring until smooth. Stir in the rosewater. Transfer the mixture to a fondue pot set over its tabletop burner to keep warm.

Serve with the almond syrup cookies and fruit for dipping.

10 oz. mascarpone cheese

¼ cup confectioners' sugar

2 tablespoons sweet Marsala wine or cream

½ teaspoon rosewater

to serve

Almond Syrup Cookies (below) or other sweet cookies

sliced fruit, such as peaches

pomegranate seeds (optional)

almond syrup cookies

8 oz. blanched almonds, toasted, 2 cups

1¼ cups sugar

finely grated zest and juice of 2 lemons

1 egg

all-purpose flour, for rolling

a baking tray, lined with parchment paper

serves 6

index

conversion charts

Weights and measures have been rounded up or down slightly to make measuring easier.

volume equivalents

American	Metric	Imperial
1 teaspoon	5 ml	
1 tablespoon	15 ml	
¼ cup	60 ml	2 fl. oz.
⅓ cup	75 ml	2½ fl. oz.
½ cup	125 ml	4 fl. oz.
⅔ cup	150 ml	5 fl. oz. (¼ pint)
¾ cup	175 ml	6 fl. oz.
1 cup	250 ml	8 fl. oz.

weight equivalents

Imperial	Metric
1 oz.	25 g
2 oz.	50 g
3 oz.	75 g
4 oz.	125 g
5 oz.	150 g
6 oz.	175 g
7 oz.	200 g
8 oz. (½ lb.)	250 g
9 oz.	275 g
10 oz.	300 g
11 oz.	325 g
12 oz.	375 g
13 oz.	400 g
14 oz.	425 g
15 oz.	475 g
16 oz. (1 lb.)	500 g
2 1b.	1 kg

measurements

Inches	Cm
¼ inch	5 mm
½ inch	1 cm
¾ inch	1.5 cm
1 inch	2.5 cm
2 inches	5 cm
3 inches	7 cm
4 inches	10 cm
5 inches	12 cm
6 inches	15 cm
7 inches	18 cm
8 inches	20 cm
9 inches	23 cm
10 inches	25 cm
11 inches	28 cm
12 inches	30 cm

oven temperatures

110°C	(225°F)	Gas ¼
120°C	(250°F)	Gas ½
140°C	(275°F)	Gas 1
150°C	(300°F)	Gas 2
160°C	(325°F)	Gas 3
180°C	(350°F)	Gas 4
190°C	(375°F)	Gas 5
200°C	(400°F)	Gas 6
220°C	(425°F)	Gas 7
230°C	(450°F)	Gas 8
240°C	(475°F)	Gas 9